FRANCE TRAVEL GUIDE

Must-See Museums, Galleries, Landmarks and Other Major Attractions

Linsley Ashley

TABLE OF CONTENT

CHAPTER ONE

Introduction: The Artistic Legacy of France.

France has long been considered as a center of culture and the arts, drawing philosophers, writers, and artists from all over the world. Everything you look at bears the mark of France's cultural past, from the refined architecture of Paris to the sun-kissed landscapes of Provence.

From Impressionists like Monet and Degas to contemporary geniuses like Picasso and Matisse, France has given birth to some of the most recognizable painters in history. Whether it was the opulence of the Baroque era or the daring experimentation of the 20th century, French art has always been a product of its time.

There are many treasures in the nation's museums and galleries, including works by Leonardo da Vinci, Vincent van Gogh, and many others. Sculpture, photography, and architecture all have a significant impact on the history of French art, which is not simply confined to paintings.

This guide will examine the must-see monuments, museums, and galleries for art lovers traveling to France. We'll take you on a tour of France's creative past and present, stopping at the Louvre, the Musée d'Orsay, Notre-Dame's gothic architecture, the Pompidou Center, and more. Discover the beauty and inventiveness that have made France a cultural powerhouse for ages as we dig into the realm of French art.

CHAPTER TWO

Paris: The Art Capital of the World.

Paris is regarded as the world's art hub for good reason. The Louvre, the Musée d'Orsay, and the Eiffel Tower are just a few of the world's most renowned museums, galleries, and sites that can be found in the city. Visitors visiting Paris can enjoy a plethora of art, from historic relics to modern masterpieces.

Any art enthusiast visiting Paris must visit the Louvre, one of the most famous museums in the world. Over 38,000 pieces, including some of history's most well-known works of art like the Mona Lisa and the Venus de Milo, are kept at the museum. Wandering the halls and taking in the beauty and range of the museum's treasures can occupy visitors for hours.

Another must-visit museum in Paris is the Musée d'Orsay, which has a sizable collection of Impressionist and Post-Impressionist works. As addition as artwork by

Monet, Van Gogh, and Renoir, visitors can also view sculptures, decorative arts, and photographs. The fact that the museum is located in a gorgeous former train station adds to the allure of the trip.

The Centre Pompidou is a must-see for anyone with an interest in modern art. The museum is home to one of Europe's largest collections of modern and contemporary art, which includes pieces by Picasso, Warhol, and Kandinsky, among others. The building itself, with its vibrant pipes and exposed construction, is also a piece of art.

Aside from museums, Paris is also the location of some well-known structures that are works of art in and of themselves. Just a few examples include Notre-Dame Cathedral, the Arc de Triomphe, and the Eiffel Tower. These landmarks are all examples of France's creative and architectural legacy.

Paris is a city that, in general, captures the creative energy of France. There is an abundance of art for visitors to explore and enjoy thanks to its top-notch museums, galleries, and landmarks.

CHAPTER THREE

The Louvre: A Comprehensive Guide to the World's Most Famous Museum.

One of the most well-known museums in the world is the Louvre, which is situated in the center of Paris. The museum is home to an amazing collection of artwork and artifacts from all around the world, including Old Master paintings and sculptures from ancient Egypt. Any art enthusiast visiting France must see the Louvre, which has over 38,000 works of art on exhibit.

The Louvre was initially a castle constructed in the late 12th century during Philip II's rule. Charles V later transformed it into a royal residence in the 14th century. The French Revolutionary period (1793–1793) saw the founding of the museum as we know it today. Only 537 artworks were kept at the museum at the time, but it has since grown to be one of the biggest in the world.

The Mona Lisa by Leonardo da Vinci is among the most well-known pieces of art on display at the Louvre. Millions of people see this tiny portrait each year, which has evolved into an icon of art. The Winged triumph of Samothrace, a Hellenistic sculpture of Nike, the Greek goddess of triumph, and the Venus de Milo, an ancient Greek sculpture of the goddess Aphrodite, are two further noteworthy items in the Louvre.

The Louvre offers a number of temporary exhibitions each year in addition to its permanent collection. These displays include artworks from the museum's collection as well as loans from other organizations throughout the globe. A number of departments and research institutions devoted to the study of art and art history are located inside the Louvre.

The vastness of the Louvre and the quantity of artwork on display might make a visit there overwhelming. It is advised that you organize your visit in advance and concentrate on the pieces or places that most interest you. To help visitors traverse the museum and learn more about its collection, audio guides and guided tours are offered.

In general, the Louvre is a must-visit location for every art enthusiast traveling to France. It is a great wonder of the art world thanks to its amazing collection and extensive history.

CHAPTER FOUR

Musée d'Orsay: The Best Collection of Impressionist Art in the World.

One of the most popular museums in Paris is the Musée d'Orsay, and it's simple to understand why. The museum's collection is focused on French art from 1848 to 1914, and it is situated in a magnificent Beaux-Arts train station that was constructed in 1900. The Impressionist and Post-Impressionist paintings in the Musée d'Orsay collection, which features pieces by some of the most well-known creators of the time, including Vincent van Gogh, Claude Monet, and Edgar Degas, are particularly well known.

The Impressionist painting collection of the museum is particularly outstanding. Some of the most well-known pieces from this time period are on display for visitors to see, including Monet's "Water Lilies," Renoir's "Dance at Le Moulin de la Galette," and Van Gogh's "Starry Night Over the Rhône." The museum's collection from that time period also includes sculptures, decorative arts, and photography.

The museum's collection of Gustave Moreau artworks, which numbers over 1,200 paintings, watercolors, and drawings, is one of its attractions. One of the most significant artists of the Symbolist movement, Moreau is recognized for his mystical and surreal elements in his works.

The Musée d'Orsay's temporary exhibitions, which include modern art by artists as well as special exhibitions on various topics pertaining to French art and culture, are also open to visitors. The museum also provides classes and guided tours for both adults and kids.

In conclusion, anyone interested in French art, particularly the Impressionist movement, must visit the Musée d'Orsay. The Musée d'Orsay is unquestionably one of the best museums in the world thanks to its magnificent Beaux-Arts construction and unrivaled collection of paintings, sculptures, and decorative arts.

CHAPTER FIVE

The Centre Pompidou: A Modern Art Museum Like No Other.

One of the most distinctive museums in the world is the Centre Pompidou, which is situated in the center of Paris. This museum is unique not only for its remarkable architectural style, which includes exposed pipes and vividly colored external escalators.

The Centre Pompidou was named after French President Georges Pompidou, who had commissioned the museum before to his passing in 1974, and it first opened its doors in 1977. Its goal was to establish a location for design, industrial development, and modern and contemporary art. The Centre Pompidou swiftly developed into a gathering place for intellectuals and avant-garde artists from all over the world.

Pablo Picasso, Salvador Dal, Henri Matisse, Andy Warhol, and other prominent modern and contemporary artists have pieces in the museum's significant permanent collection. Temporary exhibitions, which showcase a variety of artistic mediums, from sculpture to photography, are also available to visitors.

The View of Paris, which can be found on the museum's top level, is one of the most well-known sights of the Centre Pompidou. Visitors can enjoy breath-taking panoramic views of the city from here, which include the Sacré-Coeur Basilica and the Eiffel Tower.

The Centre Pompidou's focus on multidisciplinary exhibitions and events is another distinctive aspect of the institution. The museum frequently holds movie showings, musical performances, and lectures that examine the relationships between art, design, and technology. The Centre Pompidou is becoming a must-visit location for both art and culture fans thanks to its interdisciplinary approach.

The Centre Pompidou features both permanent and changing exhibitions in addition to a library, a movie theater, and a restaurant with a view of the Paris skyline. The Centre Pompidou is unquestionably a modern art museum unlike any other because to its ground-breaking architecture, remarkable collection, and wide variety of programming.

CHAPTER SIX

Musée Rodin: A Memorial to the Master Sculptor.

The Musée Rodin is a museum devoted to the creations of the renowned French sculptor Auguste Rodin, and it is situated in the center of Paris. The museum is located in the Hôtel Biron, a chateau from the 18th century that was rebuilt especially to display Rodin's creations. Three years after Rodin's passing, the museum opened its doors in 1919, and art enthusiasts have been flocking there ever since.

Over 6,000 sculptures, 8,000 drawings, and 10,000 photographs are in the museum's collection. Unquestionably "The Thinker," one of Rodin's most recognizable sculptures, is the most well-known item in the museum. Other well-known pieces in the museum include "The Kiss" and "The Gates of Hell."

The museum offers a range of spaces for visitors to study Rodin's creations, from the serene sculpture garden outdoors to the stately halls of the Hôtel Biron. Many of Rodin's most well-known pieces may be found in the gardens, including "The Burghers of Calais," a massive sculpture of the six burghers who gave their lives to preserve the city during the Hundred Years' War.

The museum exhibits a variety of temporary exhibitions in addition to its permanent collection that highlight the creations of other artists who were influenced by Rodin's aesthetic. Visitors to these displays frequently gain a clearer knowledge of Rodin's artistic legacy.

In general, Musée Rodin is a must-visit location for art enthusiasts traveling to Paris. With its beautiful gardens, outstanding collection of sculptures, and drawings. The French sculptor Auguste Rodin's creations are the focus of the Musée Rodin. It is situated inside the Hôtel Biron, where Rodin spent many years living and working, in Paris's 7th arrondissement.

A sizable collection of Rodin's sculptures, paintings, and photographs, as well as pieces by other artists who were influenced by his work, can be found in the museum. "The Thinker," which features a man lost in thought and has come to represent philosophy and introspection, is one of the most well-known pieces in the collection.

The museum exhibits numerous other well-known works by Rodin in addition to "The Thinker," including "The Kiss," "The Burghers of Calais," and "The Gates of Hell."

CHAPTER SEVEN

Musée de l'Orangerie: Residence to Monet's Water Lilies.

Any art fan visiting Paris must pay a visit to the Musée de l'Orangerie. A spectacular collection of Impressionist and Post-Impressionist paintings, including some of Claude Monet's most well-known pieces, can be seen in this modest museum in the center of the city.

Unquestionably, Monet's Water Lilies, a collection of eight monumental paintings produced in the latter years of the artist's life, is the highlight of the Musée de l'Orangerie. These breath-taking canvases are on exhibit in two oval-shaped chambers that Monet himself created specifically to display his art.

In person, the Water Lilies paintings are very gorgeous. Standing in the center of the oval-shaped rooms and being encircled by the paintings is a memorable experience because to Monet's use of color and light.

The Musée de l'Orangerie is home to an exceptional collection of works by renowned Impressionist and Post-Impressionist artists, including as Renoir, Cézanne, Matisse, and Picasso, in addition to the Water Lilies. The museum's changing exhibits, which feature a variety of modern and contemporary works of art, are also open to visitors.

The Louvre and other significant Parisian landmarks are easily accessible from the Tuileries Gardens, where the Musée de l'Orangerie is situated. The museum is open every day, and to skip the lineups, visitors can buy tickets online in advance. Any art enthusiast visiting Paris must go there, and the Water Lilies alone are worth the journey.

CHAPTER EIGHT

Musée Marmottan Monet: The Largest Collection of Monet's Works in the World.

The world's largest collection of paintings by French impressionist Claude Monet can be found in the Musée Marmottan Monet in Paris. The collection of the museum was given to the French government by Monet's son Michel in 1966, and it has since expanded to include works by other impressionist artists.

The museum is located in a stunning mansion from the 19th century that was formerly owned by a powerful art collector. It is situated close to the Bois de Boulogne in Paris' 16th arrondissement. Impressionist artwork from the museum looks beautiful against the mansion's magnificent interiors.

Over 100 Monet pieces, including some of his most well-known paintings, are part of the museum's collection. The water lily paintings by Monet that he created at his

Giverny house serve as the collection's focal point. Several of these paintings are on show in the museum, notably the enormous "Water Lilies" triptych that fills a full wall.

The museum features an excellent collection of paintings by other impressionist artists in addition to Monet's creations. Among others, the collection features pieces by Auguste Renoir, Camille Pissarro, Berthe Morisot, and Edgar Degas.

The museum's collection's emphasis on Monet's later years is among its most intriguing features. A large portion of the paintings on display were painted by Monet when he was in his 70s and 80s and had already started to lose his vision. These paintings exhibit Monet's ongoing invention and ingenuity even in his latter years. They are distinguished by their powerful, expressive brushstrokes and their vibrant colors.

The library of the Musée Marmottan Monet is home to the museum's collection of rare books and illuminated manuscripts from the Middle Ages. A highlight of any visit is the museum's garden with its magnificent pond and serene ambiance.

All things considered, the Musée Marmottan Monet is a must-visit for every admirer of impressionist artwork and offers an enthralling look into the life and career of one of the greatest painters of all time.

CHAPTER NINE

Château de Versailles: The Palace of the Sun King and Its Artistic Treasures.

One of the grandest palaces in the world is Château de Versailles, which is situated in the western suburbs of Paris. The palace was the hub of French political and cultural life for more than a century when it was built by Louis XIV, the "Sun King," in the 17th century. Attracting millions of tourists each year, it is currently one of France's most popular tourist destinations.

While the palace itself is a work of beauty, it also houses numerous museums that display the artistic treasures of the royal collections in addition to thousands of paintings, sculptures, and decorative arts.

The Galerie des Glaces, also known as the Hall of Mirrors, is one of the most well-known museums in the Château de Versailles. This gorgeous hall has 17 mirror-covered arches that reflect the outside light to amazing effect. The Treaty of Versailles' signing is one of many significant events in French history that are depicted in paintings and sculptures that line the walls of the hall.

The palace also serves as the home of the Musée de l'Histoire de France, which holds a sizable collection of artworks that record France's history from prehistoric times to the present. The artwork of well-known French artists including Jacques-Louis David, Jean-Auguste-Dominique Ingres, and Eugène Delacroix is among the museum's attractions.

The Château de Versailles also contains a number of gardens and parks that are works of art on their own, in addition to the museums. The almost 800 hectare Gardens of Versailles, which André Le Nôtre created in the 17th century, are regarded as one of the pinnacles of French landscaping. Anyone visiting the palace should spend some time in the grounds, which are full of statues, fountains, and other works of art.

The Grand Trianon, a palace constructed by Louis XIV as a refuge from the main palace, is another notable feature of the Château de Versailles. A masterwork of French architecture and design, the Grand Trianon is home to a number of museums that display the fine and applied arts of the French court.

In general, the Château de Versailles is a place that art enthusiasts must see. It ranks among the most spectacular cultural icons in the world thanks to its stunning architecture, top-notch museums, and magnificent gardens. A visit to the Château de Versailles is an extraordinary experience, whether you are interested in the art of the French court or simply want to experience the luxury and grandeur of one of the most famous castles in the world.

CHAPTER TEN

Musée Picasso: A Comprehensive Collection of the Master's Works.

If you're an art enthusiast visiting Paris, you must visit the Musée Picasso. One of the world's largest collections of Picasso's artwork is housed in this museum, which is situated in the city's Marais neighborhood. Picasso's complete body of work is represented in the museum's collection of more over 5,000 paintings, sculptures, sketches, and prints.

The museum is located in the Hôtel Salé, a magnificent mansion from the 17th century that underwent renovation in the 1980s to make room for the museum's collection. Picasso's vibrant and vivid artwork is the perfect complement to the building's opulent interiors.

Picasso's paintings, from his early Blue and Rose eras to his later Cubist and Surrealist works, are represented in the museum's collection. Some of Picasso's most well-known works are on display for visitors, including Les Demoiselles d'Avignon, a revolutionary piece that contributed to the development of the Cubist style. Picasso's sculptures are also widely represented in the museum, including his well-known bronze Bull's Head, which was created using the seat and handlebars of a bicycle.

The way the museum's collection depicts the development of Picasso's art throughout time is among its most fascinating features. Visitors can observe how his style evolved as he explored new artistic movements and tried out various approaches. The museum also houses a collection of pieces by other creatives, like Cézanne, Matisse, and Braque, who had an influence on Picasso.

The Musée Picasso also presents temporary exhibitions that highlight various facets of Picasso's art or investigate his ties with other artists in addition to its permanent collection. Recent exhibitions have included ones that highlighted Picasso's ceramics work and his partnerships with other artists.

For visitors interested in learning more about Parisian art and culture, the museum's location in the Marais neighborhood makes it a great choice. The area is renowned for its chic stores, quaint cafes, and old-world architecture. One day is certainly sufficient for tourists to thoroughly explore the region and take in its lively atmosphere.

In general, the Musée Picasso is a must-visit location for anybody interested in Pablo Picasso's work. The museum's enormous collection gives a thorough overview of his career, and its central location in Paris makes it a great place to begin exploring the many other artistic gems the city has to offer.

CHAPTER ELEVEN

Nice: The Artistic Capital of the French Riviera.

The largest city on the French Riviera, Nice is renowned for its breathtaking coastline, opulent hotels, and thriving art scene. The city's numerous museums, galleries, and public art installations reflect its long and rich history of artistic expression. We shall examine Nice's creative treasures in this chapter and discover why Nice is regarded as the French Riviera's cultural epicenter.

Henri Matisse, a French artist who is regarded as one of the most significant personalities in 20th-century art, is the subject of the museum Henri Matisse, which is devoted to his works. Besides his own collection of artwork and antiquities from Africa and the Middle East, the museum's holdings include Matisse's more than 200 paintings, sketches, sculptures, and prints.

Yves Klein, Arman, and Niki de Saint Phalle are just a few of the French painters whose works are on display at the Musée d'Art Moderne et d'Art Contemporain. Additionally, foreign artists like Andy Warhol and Roy Lichtenstein are represented here.

A National Museum Marc Chagall: The museum is home to the largest collection of the Russian-French painter Marc Chagall's works, who is well-known for his vivid, dreamy paintings. More than 400 pieces by Chagall, including paintings, sculptures, and ceramics, are included in the museum's collection.

Villa Masséna: The villa, which was constructed in the 19th century, is now a museum devoted to Nice's history and culture. The museum's collection comprises works of art from the 18th, 19th, and 20th centuries, as well as furniture, sculptures, and other decorative items.

Gallery des Ponchettes: This gallery, built in a former 17th-century stronghold, exhibits modern and contemporary works of art created by both local and foreign artists. All through the year, the gallery also offers transient exhibitions.

Promenade des Arts: The Théâtre National de Nice and the Musée d'Art Moderne et d'Art Contemporain are two of the museums and galleries that line this pedestrian route. Sculptures, murals, and mosaics are among the public art installations that can be found on the street.

Place Garibaldi: The Fontaine du Soleil, a sizable fountain constructed in the 18th century, is located in the Place Garibaldi, a public area. The Musée d'Art Naf, a gallery devoted to naïve art, is also located on the square.

Located in the center of Nice, the Jardin Albert 1er is a public park. A big fountain, many sculptures, and a variety of trees, flowers, and bushes can be seen throughout the park.

Opera de Nice: Built in the nineteenth century, the Opera de Nice is a famous opera house. Operas, ballets, and concerts are just a few of the performances that are presented in the opera house every year.

Musée des Beaux-Arts: The Musée des Beaux-Arts is a gallery that showcases decorative, fine, and applied arts. From the sixteenth to the twentieth centuries, French and European painters contributed pieces to the museum's collection.

The Cimiez Monastery is a venerable monastery that was founded in the ninth century. The monastery is now a museum that displays information about both its own and Nice's pasts.

International Museum of Native Art The naive arts of the world are showcased in this museum, according to Anatole Jakovsky. The museum's collection consists of pieces.

Nice is home to numerous stunning public artworks and structures in addition to its renowned museums. The Place Masséna, a sizable public plaza with a beautiful display of red and ochre buildings and an enormous statue of Apollo, is one of the most renowned.

The Matisse Museum, which showcases the creations of renowned French artist Henri Matisse, is yet another must-visit destination for art enthusiasts in Nice. The museum, which is housed in a stunning mansion from the 17th century in the Cimiez area, has a sizable collection of the artist's paintings, sculptures, and drawings.

The Museum of Modern and Contemporary Art (MAMAC) is a must-visit location for people who are interested in contemporary art. With a focus on Nice's post-war and contemporary art scenes, the museum features artwork from the 1950s to the present.

Last but not least, the Russian Orthodox Cathedral in Nice is a magnificent illustration of sacred art and architecture. The Russian population in Nice constructed the church in the early 20th century, and it now houses an exquisite collection of icons and frescoes.

With its stunning array of museums, public artworks, and monuments, Nice is a must-visit location for art enthusiasts. This creative hub of the French Riviera has something for everyone, from the Musée Matisse to the MAMAC.

CHAPTER TWELVE

Musée Marc Chagall: A Tribute to the Great Modernist Painter.

For fans of art, a trip to Nice's Musée Marc Chagall is a must. The famous modernist painter Marc Chagall lived his last years in the city, and the museum is devoted to his life and work. The museum's spectacular building and gardens are just as appealing as the interior artwork, and it is situated in a lovely hillside park with views of the city.

Some of Chagall's most famous pieces, including the famed ceiling mural from the Palais Garnier in Paris, are part of the museum's permanent collection. Many of Chagall's lesser-known works, including tapestries, sketches, and sculptures, are also present in the collection. The vibrant colors and surreal imagery that characterize Chagall's approach can be appreciated by visitors as they leisurely peruse the museum's exhibits.

The museum exhibits a range of temporary exhibitions all year long in addition to the permanent collection. Visitors to these exhibitions get the chance to learn more about various facets of modern art while viewing the work of other current and modern artists.

The museum's garden, which Chagall himself designed, is one of its features. The garden, which features winding walks, lush greenery, and breathtaking vistas of the surrounding hills, is a lovely fusion of Mediterranean and Russian traditions. The garden offers visitors a tranquil setting where they may stroll and enjoy the aroma of flowers and the sound of running water from the neighboring fountain.

Throughout the year, the museum also holds a number of educational programs and activities. These consist of lectures, workshops, concerts, and guided tours. Visitors can obtain a broader grasp of modern art in general as well as additional information about Marc Chagall's life and work.

Overall, everyone interested in modern art should visit the Musée Marc Chagall. Visitors of all ages will have a one-of-a-kind and wonderful experience at the museum because to its magnificent architecture, lovely gardens, and extensive collection of Chagall's work.

CHAPTER THIRTEEN

Musée Matisse: The Best Collection of Matisse's Works in the World.

For those who value the works of Henri Matisse, one of the most significant artists of the 20th century, the Musée Matisse in Nice is a must-visit. The museum has a sizable collection of his works that shows how his techniques and style have changed through time. A wide variety of paintings, sculptures, drawings, and even personal items from Matisse's life are available for viewing by visitors.

A 17th-century villa that originally served as Matisse's home now houses the Musée Matisse. Since its opening in 1963, the museum has become a popular destination for tourists in Nice. The collection is the greatest collection of Matisse's works in the world and contains more than 150 paintings, 130 drawings, and 60 sculptures.

The sequence of expansive paintings known as the "Nice period," which Matisse produced in the 1920s and 1930s while residing in the area, is one of the collection's highlights. These paintings exhibit Matisse's command of color and shape and capture the vivid hues and light of the Mediterranean. The well-known picture "La Danse," which was commissioned by Russian industrialist Sergei Shchukin and is regarded as one of Matisse's greatest masterpieces, is another noteworthy piece in the collection.

The Musée Matisse also holds temporary exhibitions that highlight the works of other artists who have been influenced by Matisse in addition to the permanent collection. Visitors to these shows gain a deeper grasp of the master painter's aesthetic heritage and the ways in which his creations have influenced numerous generations of artists.

The museum is situated in Nice's Cimiez district, a former Roman colony that is now a residential area studded with parks and gardens. Taking the bus or tram from the city center will make it simple for visitors to get to the museum. The position of the museum also provides breathtaking views of the city and the surrounding hills, making it the ideal place for an afternoon stroll.

Visitors can tour more locations in Nice that are related to Matisse's life and work in addition to the museum. For instance, Matisse himself designed the Chapelle du Rosaire de Vence, a tiny chapel in a nearby town, which includes his own stained glass windows and murals. The Matisse cemetery, where the artist is interred, is also located in the Cimiez area.

In general, the Musée Matisse is a must-see location for art enthusiasts traveling to the French Riviera. It is a worthy monument to one of the most important artists of the 20th century because of its amazing collection and lovely setting.

CHAPTER FOURTEEN

Musée National Fernand Léger: A Look at the Bold and Colorful Works of the Modernist Painter.

A National Museum A famous character in modernist art, Fernand Léger, has a museum named after him in Biot, France. The museum has a sizable collection of works by Léger, including ceramics, drawings, sculptures, and paintings, giving visitors a complete picture of the artist's career.

In 1881, Fernand Léger was born in Normandy and received his art education at the Paris-based École des Arts Décoratifs. Although the Impressionists and the Fauvists had an effect on his early works, he eventually became identified with the Cubist style. The use of strong, vivid colors, simple forms, and an interest in the contemporary urban setting all served to distinguish Léger's work.

The museum's exhibits are housed in a modernist structure created by André Svetchine. Léger's interest in modernity and industrial design is reflected in the building's geometric contours and straight lines. Thematically structured museum galleries enable visitors to examine Léger's work in a variety of settings.

One of the centerpieces of the museum is its collection of Léger paintings, which exhibit his distinctive aesthetic of vivid, flat colors and streamlined forms. Thematic groupings of the paintings reveal the artist's research of a variety of themes, including the human form, nature, and machines. Léger's sculptures, which were frequently produced in conjunction with other artists and craftspeople, are also on display in the museum.

The museum holds temporary exhibitions in addition to its permanent collection that examine the work of other artists and the cultural setting in which Léger was working. A fuller understanding of Léger's work and its position in the history of modernist art is given to visitors through the educational programs offered by the museum, which include workshops, seminars, and guided tours.

Anyone interested in modernist art, namely the work of Fernand Léger, must visit the Musée National Fernand Léger. The museum's holdings provide a thorough look at the artist's life and his role in the growth of modernist art. The modern architecture of the building and the adjacent gardens also provide a lovely backdrop for viewing Léger's artwork.

CHAPTER FIFTEEN

Musée Jean Cocteau Collection Severin Wunderman: A Tribute to the Multifaceted Artist and Poet.

The Jean Cocteau Museum Collection The museum Severin Wunderman is devoted to the prolific poet and artist Jean Cocteau. This museum, which is situated in the picturesque seaside town of Menton on the French Riviera, is a must-see for fans of the arts, literature, and movies. Over 1,800 pieces of art by Jean Cocteau, including paintings, sketches, sculptures, ceramics, and tapestries, are housed in the museum's collection. It provides a fascinating look into the life and career of this renowned artist and is home to the world's largest collection of Cocteau's works.

The museum's structure is a piece of art in and of itself. The museum's exterior is built of Cor-Ten steel, which oxidizes to produce a rust-like surface and was designed by architect Rudy Ricciotti. This provides the structure a special and distinctive aspect that perfectly matches the rocky surroundings. The museum's interior is a contemporary, light-filled atmosphere that is ideal for Cocteau's artwork.

Cocteau's life and work are covered in a variety of areas that make up the collection. Cocteau's poetry is the focus of the first area, which features a variety of books, manuscripts, and images on display. Some of Cocteau's most well-known poems, including the iconic "Le Coq et l'Arlequin," can be seen by visitors in their original draft form. A selection of Cocteau's film-related posters, images, and props are included in the second part, which is devoted to his cinematic work. Visitors can view several of Cocteau's movies in the museum's screening room, including his classic "La Belle et la Bête."

Cocteau's paintings and sketches, including some of his most well-known pieces like "La Machine Infernale" and "Le Sang d'un Poète," are featured in a separate section of the museum. The museum also houses a noteworthy collection of ceramics by Cocteau, which he produced in association with the acclaimed ceramic artist Roger Capron. These sculptures, which are both attractive and useful, can be seen by visitors for their vivid colors and striking shapes.

The reproduction of Cocteau's apartment from the Villa Santo Sospir in Saint-Jean-Cap-Ferrat is one of the museum's centerpieces. For numerous years, Cocteau resided in this flat, where he also produced some of his most well-known works. The apartment offers a fascinating look into the artist's life and has been meticulously recreated with the original furnishings and decorations.

The collection of the museum is continually changing as a result of the frequent addition of new acquisitions and shows. The museum also holds temporary exhibitions that focus on various facets of Cocteau's life and work in addition to its permanent collection. "Jean Cocteau and Music" examined Cocteau's relationship with musicians like Erik Satie and Francis Poulenc, while "Jean Cocteau and the Mediterranean" examined Cocteau's fascination with the Mediterranean Sea and the French Riviera's scenery.

A singular and educational experience is visiting the Severin Wunderman Musée Jean Cocteau Collection. The museum's collection offers intriguing insight into the life and work of one of the 20th century's most influential artists, and its breathtaking setting on the French Riviera makes it a must-see for art and nature enthusiasts. The Musée Jean Cocteau Collection Severin Wunderman is a must-visit attraction whether you've been a longtime admirer of Jean Cocteau or are just curious to learn more about this intriguing artist.

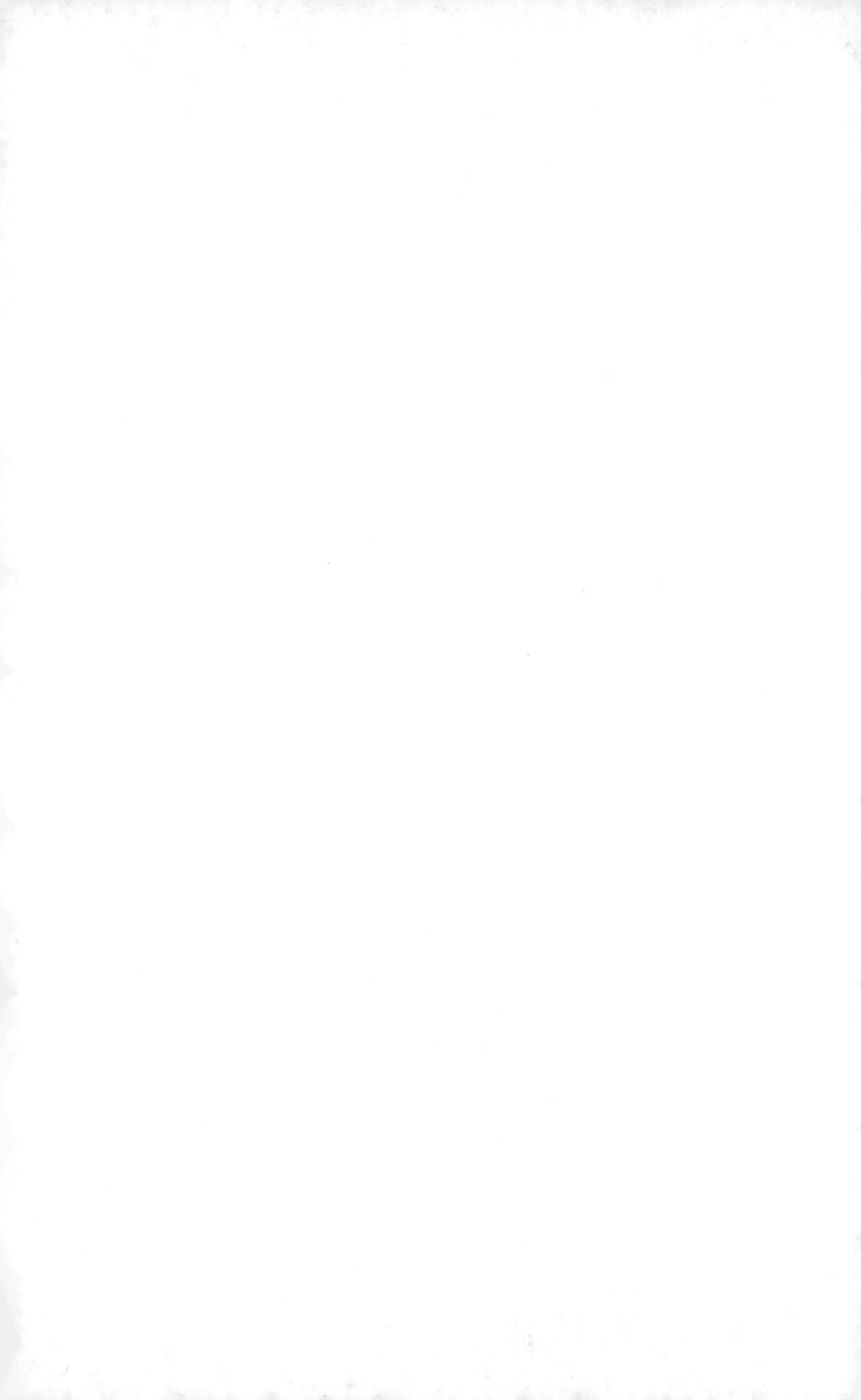